The Quick Guide to Aerial Yoga Poses

An easy picture reference guide with names for aerial yoga poses

By: Emily Griffith

Disclaimer:

By picking up this manual you are doing so to compliment previous training. This manual is not meant for you (or any individual) that has never practiced aerial yoga before. Any use or misuse of this manual is done so at your own risk. Any practice found in this manual should be done in the presence of a certified aerial yoga professional.

Consult with a healthcare professional before beginning your aerial yoga training. Aerial yoga incorporates inverts into the practice that can be harmful to individuals with certain health issues. These health issues include but are not limited to: vertigo, high or low blood pressure, recent surgery, vertigo, heart attack, or stroke.

Dear Reader,

Thanks for purchasing my Quick Guide to Aerial Yoga Poses. This guide is to be used as a 'Dictionary' for remembering your favorite poses in Aerial Yoga. This book can be used in several ways; planning classes, personal use, and aerial dance conditioning. There are three sections in this manual broke down into beginner, intermediate, and advanced poses. Each pose is broken down into the prerequisites, benefits it imposes on the body, and tips associated with the pose. Below each pose is a 'Notes' section. This is your section to write your own notes, include pose variations and sequencing ideas. Have some verbal cues you want to remind your class? Write those down here also.

To help with this manual, I have created an online video library that provides supplemental instruction of how to perform each pose, and sequencing advice.

https://www.skyaerialworks.com/aerial-yoga/

The password is:
aerialyoga30

Also, to note: I am not an author but a dancer! My goal was not to write a novel but to help others with ideas and poses for their own aerial goals. If you enjoyed this, keep an eye out for my future reference guides on restorative aerial yoga and aerial sling tricks.

I hope this manual helps you grow in your aerial yoga practice.

Love,
Emily

Beginner Poses

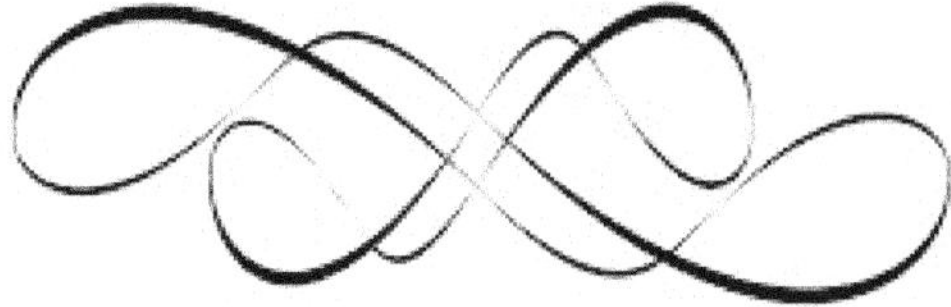

Name: *Basic Sit*

Prerequisites: None
Level: Beginner
Benefits: Balance, feeling comfortable in the hammock

Tips: Keep back straight and avoid slouching. Hold fabric just above shoulder level. Once the basic sit is mastered practice holding arms out straight behind fabric (shown in picture) and balancing in the basic sit position.

Notes:

Name: *Basic Invert*

Prerequisites: None
Level: Beginner
Benefits: spinal decompression, feeling comfortable in inverts

Tips: Keep the fabric on the lowest part of your back but off the glutes. Grab the fabric between your thumb and fingers, with your thumb closest to your body. Keep the legs out in a 'V' shape. While holding the fabric lower the upper body down, bringing the legs up and let the fabric rest against your inner thighs.

Notes:

Name: *Bucket Seat*

Prerequisites: None
Level: Beginner
Targets: Balance, feeling comfortable and balanced in the hammock

Tips: Shake out the fabric to open it up, standing in front of the fabric grab a small handful and slide it under your glutes while standing up on your toes, allowing yourself to sink into the fabric. Keep arms behind (as shown in picture) to keep an even balance.

Notes:

Name: *Seated Pike*

Prerequisites: None
Level: Beginner
Benefits: Stretches legs, back, and shoulders

Tips: Keep shoulders squared and core engaged. Try this position with pointed toes and flexed toes. Bring the knees slightly up if you are feeling too much straining.

Notes:

Name: *Hip Hang*

Prerequisites: None
Level: Beginner
Benefits: Spinal decompression, balance

Tips: Keep the fabric right below your hip bones, come up on your toes and fold over. Do not rest the fabric on your stomach, resulting to do so will cause uncomfortable pressure. Let your students know this one takes a little practice to find that comfortable resting spot of the fabric. Some will get discouraged by the discomfort.

Notes:

Name: *Hero Pose*

Prerequisites: None
Level: Beginner
Benefits: Stretches/strengthens back, strengthens knees and wrists, stretches quadriceps **Variation:** stretches obliques

Tips: Keep your feet on either side of you. Raise the chest up and bring the head down. This pose can be adjusted for students by resting your feet underneath your glutes. **Variation:** Move side to side.

Notes:

Name: *Seated Spinal Twist*

Prerequisites: Bucket Seat
Level: Beginner
Benefits: Stretches the shoulders and spine

Tips: Start in bucket seat. Bring the right hand behind the fabric reaching across your chest and grab the left fabric. Bring the left arm down and twist your upper body looking over your left shoulder. Switch arms to do this exercise on both sides.

Notes:

Name: *Pyramid Pose*

Prerequisites: none
Level: Beginner
Benefits: Strengthens and stretches legs and spine, increased shoulder flexibility, strengthens wrists

Tips: Holding the fabric at shoulder level, take one step forward with left leg. Bend elbows and drop head between both arms. Keep the shoulders squared and knees just slightly bent to prevent any over straining.

Notes:

Name: *Bow Pose*

Prerequisites: Climb into Hammock, Bucket Seat
Level: Beginner
Benefits: Back Flexibility, chest opener, stretches quads and shoulders

Tips: To get into the hammock place one knee at the back of the fabric, reach through grab the front of the fabric and slide in. Fabric should be positioned just below the shoulders to mid-thigh. Bend knees up and arch back to reach for feet behind you.

Notes:

Name: *Seated Hamstring Stretch*

Prerequisites: None
Level: Beginner
Benefits: Stretches/strengthens hamstrings

Tips: Keep the foot in the fabric flexed to hold fabric in place. Grab opposite leg behind the ankle, calf, knee, thigh, wherever is comfortable. On each exhale pull the leg slightly closer. Keep knee slightly bent to prevent strain.

Notes:

Name: *Spinal Twist*

Prerequisites: Seated Hamstring Stretch
Level: Beginner
Benefits: Stretches/strengthens hamstrings, stretches spine

Tips: If right leg is free from the fabric cross if over the left side of the body gently pushing down with your left hand. Right hand should be extended palm facing down while focusing your gaze over your right shoulder. Repeat this on both sides. This sequences well with the seated hamstring stretch.

Notes:

Name: *Stargazer*

Prerequisites: None
Level: Beginner
Benefits: Stretches back **Variation:** stretches obliques

Tips: This is a recovery pose and is great to use after inverts. Keep the fabric right below shoulder blade level. Take a few steps back and lean into the fabric. **Variation:** try bending at the waist from side to side from the stargazer position.

Notes:

Name: *Warrior II*

Prerequisites: None
Level: Beginner
Benefits: Stretches hips, opens chest, stretches/strengthens legs and ankles, strengthens shoulders

Tips: Keep the fabric behind the knee and the knee above the foot. Keep hips squared and shoulder squared. This can be done with a flexed foot or pointed toes. Extend the front arm through the center of the fabric.

Notes:

Name: *Reverse Warrior*

Prerequisites: Warrior II
Level: Beginner
Benefits: Stretches hips, opens chest, stretches/strengthens legs and ankles, stretches obliques and shoulders

Tips: Starting from a warrior II position, extend the front arm over the head, bring the back arm behind the straightened leg. **Sequence Idea**: (Inhale)-Warrior (exhale)-Reverse Warrior

Notes:

Name: *Wide Leg Forward Bend*

Prerequisites: None
Level: Beginner
Benefits: stretches legs and shoulders, Strengthens shoulders

Tips: Straddle legs, keeping knees slightly bent to prevent strain. Grab fabric and fold over dropping head below elbows.

Notes:

Name: *Cat Pose*

Prerequisites: None
Level: Beginner
Benefits: Strengthens spine, stretches hips, backs and abdomen, improves posture

Tips: Starting with our upper body parallel to the floor, and a 90* angle bend at our waist; inhale and pull the back up towards the sky creating a nice arch in upper back and shoulders, keep arms straight. (This pairs well with Cow Pose).

Notes:

Name: *Cow Pose*

Prerequisites: None
Level: Beginner
Benefits: Strengthens spine, stretches hips, backs and abdomen, improves posture

Tips: Starting with our upper body parallel to the floor, and a 90* angle bend at our waist; exhale and drop the chest down to the ground. Bend elbows and drop head between arms. (This pairs well with Cat Pose).

Notes:

Name: *Seated Childs Pose*

Prerequisites: Bucket Seat
Level: Beginner
Benefits: Stretches back and hips, relaxes upper body

Tips: From bucket seat bring arms around the outside of the fabric and gently lean forward. This is another recovery pose and great for coming out of inverts.

Notes:

Name: *Bucket Seat Invert*

Prerequisites: Bucket Seat
Level: Beginner
Benefits: spinal decompression

Tips: From Bucket Seat, 'V' the legs out and push against the fabric, lowering the upper body down. The fabric should fall just below the knees.
Note: This invert tends to be a little easier for those struggling in basic invert, due to the extra support.

Notes:

Name*:* *Hinge*

Prerequisites: None
Level: Beginner
Benefits stretches/strengthens arms, hamstrings, and shoulders, balance

Tips: Hold arms out straight bend at the waist at a 90* angle. Keep upper body parallel to the floor. Legs should about should width apart. Bringing the legs closer together will result in a deeper stretch for the hamstrings.

Notes:

Name: *Seated Straddle Bend*

Prerequisites: Bucket Seat
Level: Beginner
Benefits Stretches hamstrings and shoulders, strengthens spine, increased leg flexibility

Tips: If struggling in this position, try bending your knees upward slightly to allow yourself from overstraining. Try this with pointed toes and flexed feet to feel the difference in stretching in your hamstrings.

Notes:

Name: *Cocoon*

Prerequisites: None
Level: Beginner
Benefits: relaxation/meditation

Tips: Climb into hammock and rest on your back or get into this from bucket seat pushing the fabric to your ankles and pulling it over your head. Rest your hands on your abdomen or in prayer pose over your head. This pose is great for an end of class meditation.

Notes:

Name: *Inverted Frog*

Prerequisites: Basic Invert
Level: Beginner
Benefits: Spinal Decompression, hip and inner thigh stretch

Tips: From basic invert, bring feet in front of the fabric and to the center, hooking the toes right above the glutes.
Variation: Bring the soles of your feet together, unhooking them from the fabric in a 'prayer pose' so the bottom of the feet and all the toes are touching in the center of the fabric.

Notes:

Name: *Stand in Fabric*

Prerequisites: None
Level: Beginner
Benefits: Feeling comfortable in the fabric, strengthens arms

Tips: To avoid swinging place one foot in the fabric. Slowly raise the opposite foot of the ground without pushing into the ground. Once the foot is raised with minimum swinging, pull yourself up the rest of the way into a stand position. Hold the fabric just above should level to help with balance.

Notes:

Intermediate Poses

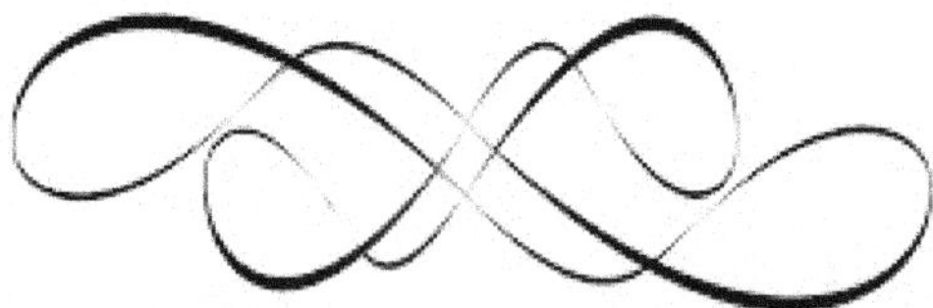

Name: *Downward Dog*

Prerequisites: Hip Hang
Level: Intermediate
Benefits: Stretches the shoulders, hamstrings, calves, arches, and hands, strengthens arms and legs

Tips: As you begin to lower yourself down into downward use your hands to keep the fabric positioned just below your hip bones. Once folded over extend arms and keep shoulders squared. Drop the chest down.

Notes:

Name: *Butterfly*

Prerequisites: Stand in Fabric
Level: Intermediate
Benefits: Strengthens back, maintains balance, strengthens shoulders, stretches hips, strengthens core

Tips: From stand in the fabric, slide down with your knees behind the fabric and soles of feet facing inward and touching. Keep arms in front, letting the fabric push up against the back of your shoulder to maintain balance.

Notes:

Name: *Flying Dancer*

Prerequisites: Stand in Fabric
Level: Intermediate
Benefits: Strengthens arms, stretches shoulders, maintains balance, strengthens core

Tips: Placing one foot in the fabric, come up to stand. Reach up high on the fabric, with the thumbs facing center. Slowly lean back pulling one foot out. Keep arms extended and drop the glutes back.

Notes:

Name: *Flying Seal*

Prerequisites: Stand in Fabric
Level: Intermediate
Benefits: Strengthens/stretches shoulders, stretches back, strengthens core and legs.

Tips: From stand in fabric raise right let up in front of you. Swing it around the outside of the right fabric bring it back into center from behind the fabric. This will create a 'lock' around your ankle. Repeat with left leg. Reach up over your head and pull shoulders out of the front of the fabric. Begin to lean forward. (Refer to video for more help).

Notes:

Name: *Half Horse*

Prerequisites: None
Level: Intermediate
Benefits: Stretches legs and hips, strengthens arms, wrists, and shoulders, increased leg flexibility

Tips: Start with the fabric in front, bring the right foot up place the fabric in the arch of the foot. Swing the foot in fabric to the right side of body. Allow the fabric to shift to your ankle. Once stable, begin to lower upper body down placing hands in front but inside the left thigh.

Notes:

Name: *Inverted Pike*

Prerequisites: basic invert
Level: Intermediate
Benefits: Spinal Decompression, stretches legs, strengthens thighs and legs

Tips: From the basic invert position (legs in the 'V' shape), begin to bring your legs together over your head. Squeeze the fabric between your thighs keeping legs straight and toes pointed.

Notes:

Name: *Splits*

Prerequisites: None
Level: Intermediate
Benefits: Stretches hamstrings, hips, and shoulders, strengthens arms and shoulders, increased leg flexibility

Tips: Keep the fabric in the arch of the foot, holding the fabric slightly above shoulder level lean forward. Drop the hips down to deepen the pose.

Notes:

Name: *Crescent Lunge*

Prerequisites: None
Level: Intermediate
Benefits: Maintain balance, stretches legs and hips, strengthens core and quads

Tips: Start standing in front of the fabric. Slide the top of your ankle in the fabric behind you. Slowly begin to push the hooked foot out straight behind you while bending the opposite knee. Keep knee above the free foot and hips squared.

Notes:

Name: *Inverted Pidgeon Pose*

Prerequisites: Basic Invert
Level: Intermediate
Benefits: Spinal Decompression, stretches hip flexors, back, and shoulders

Tips: From basic invert, bring one leg in front of the fabric and begin to bend the knee of the opposite leg behind you. Reach for the foot and begin to gently tug towards you.

Notes:

Name: *Chair Pose*

Prerequisites: Stargazer
Level: Intermediate
Benefits: Strengthens glutes, back, and hamstrings, improves posture

Tips: Start by standing in front of the fabric and placing the fabric in front of your arms like a backpack. Take a small step back and sink into the fabric allowing it to rest just below shoulder blade level. It should not be digging in your armpits. Drop glutes towards the ground and lengthen the back.

Notes:

Name: *Diaper Wrap (Straddle)*

Prerequisites: Basic Invert, Inverted Pike
Level: Intermediate
Benefits: Strengthens arms, core, shoulders, thighs, stretches thighs and back

Tips: From an inverted pike, slide feet thru the center of the fabric locking the fabric in your knees. Reach up the fabric pulling yourself up. Push down and out with your thighs into the fabric to assist in coming up into the straddle position. Once here, you can pull yourself up to adjust the fabric positioning. Keep fabric on lower back.

Notes:

Name: *Plank*

Prerequisites: Crescent Lunge
Level: Intermediate
Benefits: Hand, wrist, arm, and shoulder strength, balance, core and back strength.

Tips: From Crescent Lunge, lower hands down to the ground in front of you. Bring the free foot underneath your upper body and slide into the fabric. Keep your body parallel to the ground with core engaged and glutes tucked.

Notes:

Name: *Crochet Legs*

Prerequisites: Crescent Lunge
Level: Intermediate
Benefits: spinal decompression, strengthens thighs, stretches legs

Tips: From inverted pike position, bring feet thru the center of the fabric, hooking ankles and slowly slide the legs up, keeping the top wrap in the arch of the feet.

Notes:

Name: *Warrior III*

Prerequisites: Hinge
Level: Intermediate
Benefits: Balance, strengthens shoulders, core, and legs, stretches shoulders and legs

Tips: Practice on keeping the body parallel to the floor, keep core engaged and arms straight. **Variation:** Swimmer kick the raised leg to add an extra workout.

Notes:

Name: *Low Waterfall*

Prerequisites: Bucket Seat
Level: Intermediate
Benefits: Stretches hips, opens chest, stretches/strengthens legs and ankles, stretches obliques and shoulders

Tips: From cocoon pull upper body out and begin to lean back, let fabric fall to lower back keeping the core engaged.

Notes:

Name: *Low Lunge*

Prerequisites: None
Level: Intermediate
Benefits:
Tips:

Notes:

Name: *Flying Chair*

Prerequisites: None
Level: Intermediate
Benefits: stretches/strengthens shoulders, strengthens core, back flexibility

Tips: Before going into this pose make sure the fabric is pulled over your feet and up to your knees. Keep shoulders in. Bring legs up and over head, keep body parallel to floor.

Notes:

Name: *Bow Pose*

Prerequisites: None
Level: Intermediate
Benefits: Back Flexibility and chest opener

Tips: To get into the hammock place one knee at the back of the fabric, reach through grab the front of the fabric and slide in. Fabric should be positioned just below the shoulders to mid-thigh. Bend knees up and arch back to reach for feet behind you.

Name: *Rolling Pin*

Prerequisites: None
Level: Intermediate
Benefits: Strengthens shoulders, arms, wrists, and core

Tips: Come up on knees, hips squared over knees. Begin to lean forward keeping core engaged and arms straight. Avoid overbending the elbows and dropping the stomach to low.

Notes:

Name: *Monkey Pose*

Prerequisites: None
Level: Intermediate
Benefits: stretches/strengthens shoulders, strengthens core, back flexibility

Tips: From a seated position behind the fabric bend one leg in front and slide the other behind knee rotated towards the ground.   Grab the fabric and gently lean forward keeping arms straight and turning your gaze up towards the sky.

Notes:

Name: *Floating Boat*

Prerequisites: None
Level: Intermediate
Benefits:

Tips: Keep the fabric on the lowest part of your back.

Notes:

Advanced Poses

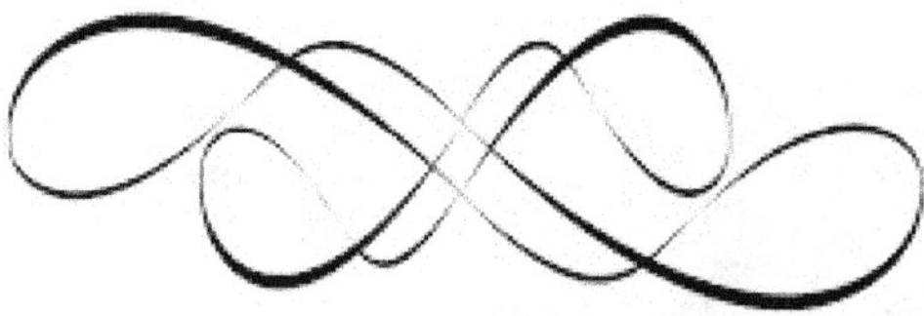

Advanced Name: *Manta Ray*

Prerequisites: Stand in Fabric
Level: Advanced
Benefits: Stretches back, maintains balance

Tips: From stand in the fabric slide, bring one leg thru center in front. Slide the foot in the loop out to the side. It will move up the fabric slightly. The key to this move is to keep the fabric on your lower back and off the butt. Keep the back slightly arched to balance (refer to video for more help).

Notes:

Name: *Flying Lotus*

Prerequisites: Hip Hang
Level: Advanced
Benefits: Strengthens core and glutes, maintains balance

Tips: From hip hang, engage the core and bring up the upper body. Hold it in this position. The fabric should be resting just below the hip bones.

Notes:

Name: *Inverted Butterfly*

Prerequisites: Butterfly Pose (shoulder strength)
Level: Advanced
Benefits: Spine decompression, full body stretch

Tips: From butterfly pose bring your body through the center of the fabric and fold over. To come out, reach arms behind, grab the fabric, and pull yourself up to butterfly pose. Coming back up is the hardest part. Feel confident in your shoulder strength before attempting this.

Notes:

Name: *Camel Pose*

Prerequisites: Chair Pose
Level: Advanced
Benefits: increase back flexibility, open chest, strengthens glutes and core

Tips: From Chair pose, raise the chest up towards the sky and drop the glutes down. Fabric should be resting at shoulder blade level. Keep legs straight and core engaged. If done correctly you will feel light stretching in your lower back.

Notes:

Name: *Liberty*

Prerequisites: Stand in Fabric
Level: Advanced
Benefits: Strengthens core, thighs and glutes, maintain balance

Tips: Keeping the right foot in the fabric bring the two poles of the fabric together inside your right thigh and keeping the fabric in front. Bring the left foot from behind the fabric to the front of the fabric and place on the inside of your right knee, lean body to the right keeping the fabric at the top of your left thigh.

Notes:

Name: *Flying Heron*

Prerequisites: Basic Sit
Level: Advanced
Benefits: Balance, increased leg flexibility, strengthens arms

Tips: Stand behind fabric and bring one leg thru the center so the fabric is resting mid-thigh. Lean forward bringing shoulders through so they rest against the front of the fabric. Raise leg thru the fabric in a pike position and slowly lower the leg behind reaching for your foot behind you.

Notes:

Name: *Dolphin Pose*

Prerequisites: Plank
Level: Advanced
Benefits: Strengthens arms, wrists, hands, shoulders, core and glutes, stretches legs

Tips: Start in plank position. Begin to raise the glutes in the air while bringing your legs towards the upper body. Keep legs straight and shoulders squared underneath your hands. Focus your gaze on your feet.

Notes:

Name: *Dancer Pose*

Prerequisites: Crescent Lunge
Level: Advanced
Benefits: Strengthens core, increases back and leg flexibility, stretches shoulders

Tips: Stand in front of the fabric and hook the top of the ankle in the fabric behind you. Reach your arms up grab the fabric above your head, thumbs face down and lean forward, pulling your leg up. Push against the fabric with the same foot. Focus your gaze down and out to help maintain balance.

Notes:

Name: *King Pidgeon Pose*

Prerequisites: Straddle, Crochet leg
Level: Advanced
Benefits: Strengthens arms, increases back and leg flexibility

Tips: Start with one crochet leg and one ankle in front of the fabric, push the crochet leg out, keeping the fabric in the arch of the foot. Keep the other ankle against your torso. To come out unhook ankle of crocheted leg and go into straddle. (this might take practice, refer to How-to-Video for more help.

Notes:

Name: *Reverse Plank*

Prerequisites: Plank
Level: Advanced
Benefits: stretches shoulders, strengthens core, back, glutes, wrists, and arms

Tips: Start in Plank and begin rotating to one side keeping your feet in the fabric. Once completely rotated focus on keeping core engaged and body parallel to the floor. Thumbs should be faced out and hands squared under shoulders.

Notes:

Name: *Pike in the Air*

Prerequisites: Chair Pose
Level: Advanced
Benefits: Spinal Decompression, Strengthens Hip Flexors, quads, and glutes, core, and arms, stretches legs

Tips: Start in Chair Pose. Once the fabric is comfortably positioned at the shoulder blades begin to raise both legs, keeping them straight and grabbing with your hands behind your thigh.

Notes:

Name: *Iron T*

Prerequisites: Stand in Loop, (wrist strength)
Level: Advanced
Benefits: Strengthens, shoulders, arms, wrists, and hands

Tips: Start from stand in fabric. Bring your shoulders and arms in front. Take your arms around the outside of the fabric and thru the center from behind so your thumbs are face down. Slowly and simultaneously begin the raise of the fabric and lift your feet. If you begin to feel to much straining in your wrist step your feet back into the fabric and release the pose.

Notes:

Name: *Elbow Stand*

Prerequisites: Basic Invert, Basic Sit

Level: Advanced

Benefits: Strengthens, arms, shoulders, core, glutes, and quads, maintains balance stretches back

Tips: From basic sit, slide the glutes back and slide the fabric underneath the knees. Hold on to the fabric and lower your upper body down resting on forearms. One foot at a time slide the fabric from your knee to the arch of the foot. To come out, slide the fabric back behind the knee and pull yourself up to sit.

Notes:

Name: *One Legged Dog*

Prerequisites: Downward Dog

Level: Advanced

Benefits: Stretches shoulders, arms and back, increased leg flexibility

Tips: Bring the leg around the outside of the fabric and through the center, hooking foot just above the glutes. To deep the pose, slide hooked ankle up the fabric to straighten out the leg.

Notes:

Name: *Inverted Bow*

Prerequisites: Bucket Seat

Level: Advanced

Benefits: Strengthens core, increased back flexibility, stretches back, shoulders, and thighs

Tips: Start in Bucket Seat. Begin to lean back extending the arms and reaching underneath the fabric for your feet. Keep the core engaged. It is normal to feel the fabric slide from mid back to lower back.

Notes:

About the Author

My name is Emily Ann, and I am a teacher, student, and performer of the aerial arts. aerial yoga has been my foundation for practicing aerial dance. It has helped in all aspects of increasing flexibility and gaining strength. Creating this guide allowed me to share some of my favorite poses I have used in my training. The money made from this book will go towards website maintenance and funding my own studio someday.

My Life Outside Dance isn't any less active! I was born and raised in Cleveland Ohio and hold a bachelor's degree in biology from Cleveland State University. I have three kids and to many pets. We spend our free time camping, fishing, and just any activity that involves being outdoors.

I am currently teaching at a studio in
Cleveland and offer classes in aerial yoga, aerial sling, aerial silks, lyra, and lollipop.
I specialize in adult and kid classes. Private lessons, bookings, performances are
always available. Email me: skyaerialworks@gmail.com

Website: *Skyaerialworks.com*

Be on the lookout for my next reference guides:
- *Aerial Sling Tricks*
- *Restorative Aerial Yoga*